Title: The Amazing Lewis
R.L.: 5.2
PTS: 0.5
TST: 189869

Fact Finders®

Landmarks in U.S. History

THE AMAZING LEWIS AND CLARK EXPEDITION

by Jean F. Blashfield

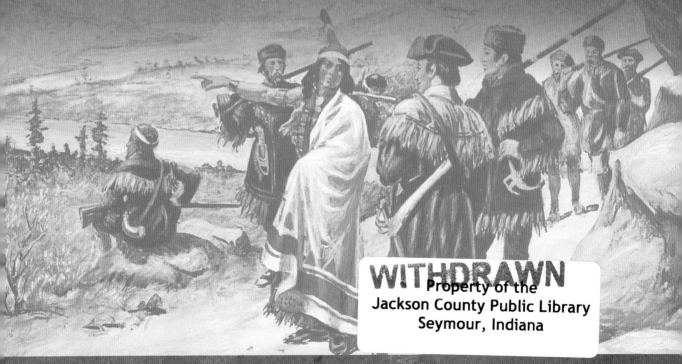

CAPSTONE PRESS
a capstone imprint

Fact Finder Books are published by Capstone Press,
1710 Roe Crest Drive, North Mankato, Minnesota 56003
www.mycapstone.com

Library of Congress Cataloging-in-Publication Data
Names: Blashfield, Jean F., author.
Title: The Amazing Lewis and Clark Expedition / by Jean F. Blashfield.
Description: North Mankato, Minnesota : Capstone Press, [2017] | Series: Fact
    finders. Landmarks in U.S. history | Includes index. | Includes
    bibliographical references and index. | Audience: Grades 4–6. | Audience: Ages 8–10.
Identifiers: LCCN 2017003800 (print) | LCCN 2017004632 (ebook) |
    ISBN 9781515771203 (library hardcover) | ISBN 9781515771418 (paperback) |
    ISBN 9781515771456 (eBook PDF)
Subjects: LCSH: Lewis and Clark Expedition (1804–1806)—Juvenile literature.
    | West (U.S.)—Discovery and exploration—Juvenile literature. | West
    (U.S.)—Description and travel—Juvenile literature.
Classification: LCC F592.7 .B54 2017 (print) | LCC F592.7 (ebook) | DDC
    917.804/2—dc23
LC record available at https://lccn.loc.gov/2017003800

Editorial Credits
Bradley Cole and Gena Chester, editors; Sarah Bennett and Brent Slingsby, designers;
Pam Mitsakos, media researcher; Steve Walker, production specialist

Photo Credits
Bridgeman Images: Baraldi, Severino/Private Collection/© Look and Learn, 29, Paxson, Edgar Samuel/
Private Collection/Peter Newark American Pictures, 18; Getty Images: Bettmann, cover, 1, 11, 21,
Ed Vebel, 12–13, Florilegius/SSPL, 15 top left; Granger Historical Picture Archive: Granger, NYC, 23;
National Geographic Creative: Stanley Meltzoff/Silverfish Press, 8–9; North Wind Picture Archives:
17, 28, Nancy Carter, 27; Shutterstock: Craig Hanson, 6–7 background, Everett Historical, 7 top left,
7 middle right, Faenkova Elena, 15 middle right, KUCO, 15 bottom left, Nagel Photography, 24–25,
Tischenko Irina, 15 background; XNR Productions: XNR/Map, 5

Design Elements:
Shutterstock: Andrey_Kuzmin, ilolab, Jacob J. Rodriguez-Call, Jessie Eldora Robertson, Olga Rutko

Printed and bound in the USA
010399F17

TABLE OF CONTENTS

A YOUNG NATION

In 1803, Thomas Jefferson, author of the Declaration of Independence, became the third president of the United States. He was an intelligent president eager for the nation to grow. Known as a "man of the people," Jefferson was well liked by most Americans.

The United States bought a large piece of land from France on April 30, 1803. The $15 million deal was called the Louisiana Purchase. It included land west of the Mississippi River to the Rocky Mountains. The new land stretched south from the Gulf of Mexico and north to the Canadian border. The United States had only been **independent** for 27 years. The Louisiana Purchase doubled the young country's size.

DID YOU KNOW?

Jefferson had planned to spend up to $10 million for Louisiana and west Florida. Although he ended up spending more than he planned, the purchase was a great success. The Louisiana Purchase made up all or part of what would become 15 states.

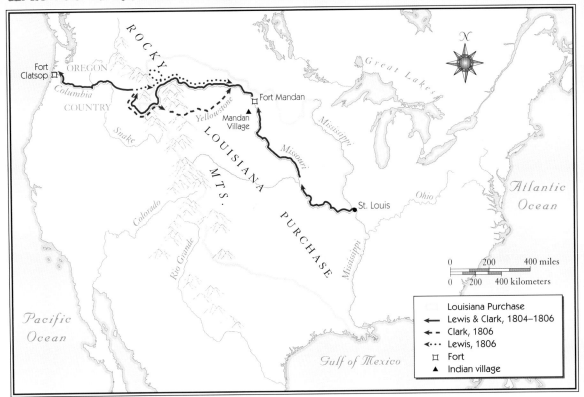

Jefferson had big plans for the nation's new land. He wanted an **expedition** to explore the area to see if there was a water route between the Mississippi River and the Pacific Ocean. If a water route existed, American traders could more easily travel west to increase trade across the Pacific Ocean.

....

independent—free from the control of other people or things
expedition—a group of people on a journey

Jefferson also hoped that the land west of the Rocky Mountains, called the Oregon Territory, would someday belong to the United States. The nation's borders would then reach from the Atlantic Ocean to the Pacific Ocean. With all that land, the United States would surely become a great and powerful nation.

Crossing thousands of miles of unmapped land and dealing with American Indians would present great challenges. The expedition would be called the Corps of Discovery. Jefferson needed smart, brave people to lead the expedition.

Jefferson chose his personal secretary, Meriwether Lewis, to head the Corps of Discovery. Lewis was a former U.S. Army officer and a skilled outdoorsman. He was honored to be chosen and eager to begin the trip. Lewis asked his best friend, William Clark, to join him. Clark also had served in the U.S. Army and had experience in the wilderness.

Meriwether Lewis

William Clark

PREPARING FOR THE EXPEDITION

Lewis and Clark set up camp on the Mississippi River near St. Louis, Missouri, in the winter of 1803. Lewis, Clark, and their group of about 40 men began training and planning for the trip, which wouldn't begin until the next year. They built boats, exercised, and practiced shooting. They packed supplies, including food, medicine, tools, and rifles.

DID YOU KNOW?

The oldest of the Corps of Discovery men was 35. The youngest was about 17. The average age of the men in the Corps of Discovery was 27.

the Corps of Discovery crossing a river

They prepared for the dangers that lay ahead, including the many American Indian tribes they would **encounter**. If members of the expedition could make friends with them, the American Indians might share their knowledge of the land. So the explorers packed gifts, such as beads, mirrors, pipes, knives, handkerchiefs, and belts.

Members of the expedition knew about hunting, steering down rivers, **blacksmithing**, making guns and bullets, and surviving in the wilderness. There was only one African-American man on the expedition. His name was York. He was William Clark's slave.

York

York was born in November 1770 in Carolina County, Virginia. He became the slave of William Clark around the age of 15. Clark's family and York moved to Kentucky in the 1780s.

York greatly contributed to the expedition by cooking, scouting, and hunting for game. Clark gave York his freedom sometime after 1815. He also gave him a wagon and horses, which York used to start a hauling business. But the business eventually failed. It is thought that York died between 1822 and 1832 of **cholera**.

encounter—an unexpected or difficult meeting

blacksmithing—heating and hammering iron

cholera—a dangerous disease that causes severe sickness and diarrhea

THE START OF THE EXPEDITION

The Lewis and Clark expedition left St. Louis on May 14, 1804. The men traveled in three boats. The largest was a 55-foot- (17-meter-) long keelboat with one sail. A keelboat is a large wooden riverboat with a cabin built in the center. Twenty-two men were needed to row. The team had two other boats — a **pirogue** and canoe.

The trip was expected to take about a year and a half. The group planned to travel northwest along the Missouri River. They hoped to reach the Rocky Mountains by the winter of 1804, which was at the time seven months away. From there they would cross what they thought was a short pass to the Columbia River. This would lead them to the Pacific Ocean by spring 1805. They planned to be back in St. Louis by the fall of 1805.

pirogue—a canoelike boat

the Corps of Discovery on a keelboat

Northwest travel along the Missouri River turned out to be more difficult than the leaders expected. They were constantly attacked by mosquitoes and ticks. Only the smoke from campfires and smearing themselves with grease helped solve these problems.

Both Clark and Lewis were excellent leaders and outdoorsmen. Clark loved to talk and tell jokes. He usually **supervised** the boats. Lewis was a serious man and sometimes suffered from **depression**. He often preferred to be alone. Lewis walked and explored the banks of the Missouri River with his dog, Seaman.

By August the expedition had reached what would become South Dakota. The **plains** were filled with buffalo. The men hunted and ate their first buffalo on August 23. They also enjoyed turkeys, geese, beaver, and fish.

Lewis and Clark kept detailed records for President Jefferson. They wrote about the land, American Indians, weather, animals, plants, and the attitudes of the men. The animals of the plains included coyotes, prairie dogs, and jackrabbits. A type of goat called a **pronghorn** — creatures that the men had never seen before — also lived there.

---

supervise—to watch over or direct a group of people

depression—an emotional disorder that causes people to feel sad and tired

plain—a large, flat area of land with few trees

pronghorn—an animal of western North America that looks like an antelope and can run very quickly

DISCOVERIES OF LEWIS AND CLARK

178 PLANTS

122 ANIMALS

50 AMERICAN INDIAN TRIBES

During the expedition, Lewis and Clark noted at least 202 new species of plants and animals that they had never seen before, including the grizzly bear.

MEETING AMERICAN INDIANS

The expedition met some Otoe and Missouria people in August. They were among the Plains Indians who lived in the large grassland region. The Otoe and Missouria were friendly.

However, the explorers soon met the Sioux, who were not friendly. Even President Jefferson's message of peace **offended** them. The Sioux accepted the gifts the explorers brought, but the gifts caused problems too.

One Sioux chief felt he was not offered enough, and he tried to take one of the expedition's boats. One hundred Sioux stood on shore and pointed arrows at the explorers. Lewis ordered his men to aim their guns at the Sioux. The American Indians backed down and left.

By November the explorers were in what would become central North Dakota, home of the Mandan people. The Mandan were welcoming and pleased with the explorers' gifts. The two groups became friends and smoked a peace pipe together.

As the cold winter approached, the explorers decided to stay in North Dakota until spring. They built a fort and called it Fort Mandan. During the winter months, the explorers learned about the America Indians' way of life and the land ahead.

offend—to make someone feel upset or angry

sacred—holy or having to do with religion

The Lewis and Clark expedition left Fort Mandan in April 1805. Toussaint Charbonneau, a French-Canadian fur trapper who lived among the American Indians, joined the expedition. He and his wife Sacagawea would guide the explorers through the mountains. They also would help with communication with other American Indians.

Sacagawea leading Lewis and Clark

Sacagawea

When Sacagawea was about 12 years old, she was kidnapped by enemy Hidatsas. The Hidatsa were connected to the Mandan. The Hidatsa enslaved her and took her to their village near present day Bismarck, North Dakota. There she was bought by Toussaint Charbonneau, a Canadian fur trader. She became one of his two wives.

Lewis and Clark met Charbonneau and Sacagawea at the Hidatsa-Mandan village in 1804. The explorers correctly thought the two might be of help to them. Charbonneau spoke French, and Sacagawea spoke Hidatsa and Shoshone.

After the expedition in 1809, Sacagawea and Charbonneau went to St. Louis to visit Clark. He had offered to educate their son, Baptiste. Clark became his gaurdian two years later.

In 1812 Sacagawea gave birth to a daughter, Lisette. Soon after Sacagawea died from an illness. Clark eventually became guardian to Lisette as well.

Sacagawea was an 18-year-old Shoshone girl. The Shoshone lived near the Rocky Mountains and had many horses. The men hoped Sacagawea would help the expedition get the horses they needed from the Shoshone. As it turned out, Sacagawea greatly helped the Corps of Discovery in many ways.

On May 14, 1805, exactly one year into their trip, a storm came up suddenly. Charbonneau panicked, and one of the pirogues almost overturned. Sacagawea stayed calm and saved the items that had washed overboard.

DID YOU KNOW?
Sacagawea's 2-month-old baby boy, Jean Baptiste, nicknamed Pomp, joined the expedition too.

A FORK IN THE RIVER

The group came to a **fork** in the Missouri River on June 3, 1805. One half of the river went south. The other went north. All around them, they saw large green plains with herds of buffalo, elk, antelopes, and wolves. They could also see mountains, some of which were covered with snow. But even with this view, they were unsure which river to take. From talking with their American Indian friends, they knew they had to continue on the Missouri River. But which river was the Missouri? To help them decide, Lewis and Clark set out to study the south and north rivers. Lewis explored the north river, and Clark explored the south.

Finally, after much thought, Lewis and Clark chose a direction. They reached the Great Falls in Montana around June 13. They had chosen correctly. The region was familiar to Sacagawea, who had once lived on this land. The explorers could not take the boats through the falls. Instead, they used cottonwood and willow trees to build trucks with wheels to carry the boats over land. It took about a month to get through the falls.

— ALFRED RUSSELL

DID YOU KNOW?
The Lewis and Clark expedition often came across wild animals. A brown bear once chased Lewis for 80 yards (73 m). Lewis finally ran into the river, and the bear decided not to follow him.

Soon after, Sacagawea became dangerously sick. Clark nursed her back to health. Lewis also became very ill and boiled the twigs of a plant he described as the "choke cherry." After only two doses of the strong dark liquid, Lewis's fever went down, and he was no longer in pain.

fork—a place where a river splits into two or more directions

The expedition came to another turning point in the Missouri River in August 1805. There the Missouri split into three rivers — an area the team called Three Forks. Again, a decision had to be made. They chose the largest river and named it the Jefferson. At times the rapids were so strong that they had to carry the canoes.

The group finally reached a stretch of high ground called the **Continental Divide**. At this point, rivers on the west flow to the Pacific Ocean. On the other side of the divide, rivers flow east to the Mississippi.

Finally the party met Sacagawea's people, the Shoshone. She was overjoyed to find that her brother, Cameahwait, was the chief. Having Sacagawea in the group was a sign of peace to the Shoshone since women were never part of warrior groups that were ready to fight. Passage through the Rocky Mountains was not possible by water. Cameahwait sold the expedition the horses they needed to cross the dangerous mountain landscape.

Continental Divide—the stretch of high ground formed by the crests of the Rocky Mountains; rivers on the east of it flow to the Atlantic Ocean and rivers on the west flow to the Pacific Ocean

As the explorers began the crossing in late September 1805, the weather worsened. Snow, freezing rain, and lack of animals to hunt made the journey even more difficult. Sacagawea's knowledge of which roots to eat was helpful, but the men were starving. At times they had to shoot their horses and mules for meat.

the Corps of Discovery crossing the Rocky Mountains

At last they finished their journey through the Rocky Mountains. They built five **dugout canoes**, as they had been taught by the American Indians, and entered the Snake River. Things improved as the river grew wider and gentler. The men were able to catch salmon, and animals were plentiful. The explorers ate well and regained their strength.

The expedition had now entered the Oregon Territory. The area was not part of the United States. But Lewis and Clark's exploration of the region caused the United States to claim it.

The Snake River turned into the Columbia River, which emptied into the Pacific Ocean. The Lewis and Clark expedition finally saw the Pacific Ocean on November 7, 1805. The men were filled with happiness and relief. They had reached their **destination**.

DID YOU KNOW?
Starting in 1841, more than 200,000 Americans moved to the Oregon Territory. Inspired by Lewis and Clark's expedition, many people left their homes for a new beginning in Oregon. These settlers created what would become known as the "Oregon Trail."

dugout canoe—a canoe made by hollowing out a large log

destination—the place to which one is traveling

Fort Clatsop

The group chose a place to build a camp for the winter. They called it Fort Clatsop, after the American Indians who lived nearby. The explorers stayed through the winter — more than four months. They finally packed up and began the return trip by land on March 23, 1806.

THE RETURN TRIP

The expedition followed most of its previous route on the way home. But after the Rocky Mountains, Lewis and Clark split up to explore different routes. Clark followed what is now called the Yellowstone River. Lewis took the unexplored Marias River to the north. They met back at the Missouri River, and completed their journey home together.

When the expedition reached the Mandan village in North Dakota, Sacagawea and Charbonneau decided to stay. Much of the expedition's success had been because of Sacagewea. Her son, Pomp, was now more than a year old. Everyone had grown to love Sacagawea and her family and would miss them.

Marias River joining the Missouri River

The expedition finally returned to St. Louis on September 23, 1806. Huge crowds came to welcome them home. After nearly two and a half years, everyone had thought they were dead. The Lewis and Clark expedition had survived everything, including bad weather, starvation, illnesses, and contact with more than 50 American Indian tribes. They had traveled dangerous land and water crossings. Amazingly, the expedition had lost only one member of its team. Sergeant Charles Floyd died of an illness three months into the journey.

The expedition traveled more than 7,689 miles (12,372 kilometers). It was a disappointment that a water route all the way to the Pacific Ocean did not exist. However, the journals Lewis and Clark kept were priceless. They had made excellent maps as well as sketches of the land, rivers, plants, and animals.

Lewis and Clark led the greatest expedition in early American history. It paved the way for fur trappers, **mountaineers**, and settlers to go west. The United States had a claim to the land west of the Rocky Mountains. And a stronger and wealthier United States stretched from the Atlantic Ocean all the way to the Pacific Ocean — "from sea to shining sea."

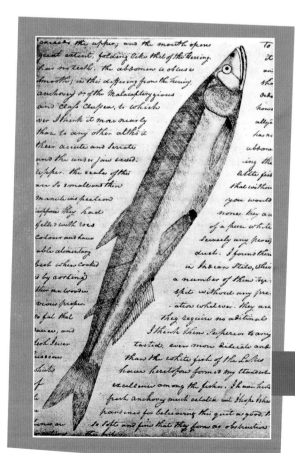

William Clark's notes and a sketch of a salmon

mountaineer—a mountain climber

John Colter

American trapper and explorer John Colter is credited as the first white man to have seen and described what is now Yellowstone National Park.

Colter was a member of Lewis and Clark's expedition from 1803 to 1806. He left the expedition at Mandan when he joined a trapping party led by Manuel Lisa. While in the party, Colter explored the area around the Rocky Mountains. He reported seeing the hot springs and geysers of Yellowstone. Many began calling the area "Colter's Hell."

On his journeys Colter had many dangerous run-ins with American Indians. He barely escaped with his life after one encounter with the Blackfeet. He is remembered as a hero among trappers, traders, and mountaineers.

GLOSSARY

blacksmithing (BLAK-smith-ing)—heating and hammering iron

cholera (KAH-luhr-uh)—a dangerous disease that causes severe sickness and diarrhea

Continental Divide (KAHN-tuh-nuhntl di-VIDE)—the stretch of high ground formed by the crests of the Rocky Mountains; rivers on the east of it flow to the Atlantic Ocean and rivers on the west flow to the Pacific Ocean

depression (di-PRE-shuhn)—an emotional disorder that causes people to feel sad and tired

destination (des-tuh-NAY-shuhn)—the place to which one is traveling

dugout canoe (DUHG-out kuh-NOO)—a canoe made by hollowing out large logs

encounter (en-KOUN-ter)—an unexpected or difficult meeting

expedition (ek-spuh-DI-shuhn)—a group of people on a journey

fork (FORK)—a place where a river splits into two or more directions

independent (in-di-PEN-duhnt)—free from the control of other people or things

mountaineer (moun-tuh-NIHR)—a mountain climber

offend (uh-FEND)—to make someone feel upset or angry

pirogue (PEE-rohg)—a canoelike boat

plain (PLAYN)—a large, flat area of land with few trees

pronghorn (PRONG-horn)—an animal of western North America that looks like an antelope and can run very quickly

sacred (SAY-krid)—holy or having to do with religion

supervise (SOO-pur-vize)—to watch over or direct a group of people

CRITICAL THINKING QUESTIONS

1. Why were expeditions such as Lewis and Clark's so important to the United States?

2. The Lewis and Clark expedition reached high ground known as the Continental Divide. What is significant about the Continental Divide?

3. How would Lewis and Clark's journey gone differently without Sacagawea's help?

READ MORE

Edwards, Judith. *The Journey of Lewis and Clark in United States History.* In United States History. Berkeley Heights, N.J.: Enslow Publishers, Inc., 2015.

Levy, Jane. *Lewis and Clark in Their Own Words.* Eyewitness to History. New York: Gareth Stevens Publishing, 2014.

Micklos, John. *Discovering the West.* Adventures on the American Frontier. North Mankato, Minn.: Capstone Press, 2015.

INTERNET SITES

Use Facthound to find Internet sites related to this book.

Visit *www.facthound.com*

Just type in 9781515771203 and go!

 Check out projects, games and lots more at
www.capstonekids.com

INDEX